★ FOR M

女儿是父母的万花筒

365 Daily Messages of Love

[英]帕姆·布朗 —— 著

新星出版社　NEW STAR PRESS

January

January

My daughter, totally yourself. Bright as a button and eager for the world.

我的女儿是一个拥有独立灵魂的个体，活泼可爱，对这个世界充满了好奇。

January 2

How could I ever have anticipated the joy you have given me?

我从未料到你能给我带来如此大的快乐。

3 January

Surprises. Amazement. She is your diamond daughter. She can cut across your heart and mind.

她是我无尽惊喜的源泉,是我的掌上明珠。我的心里眼里,全部是她。

January 4

In you my life begins again. 有了你,我仿佛重获新生。

January 5

Like it or not, we are bound to one another. It is the lightest of links – so light that sometimes we seem to forget it altogether. But it is stronger than life itself.

命运从未问过我们的选择,就这样将我们连接在一起。这血缘的纽带看不见、摸不着,虚无到似乎可以忘记,但事实上,它极强大、极坚韧,能经受住生活中所有的磨砺。

January 6

A loving daughter is the most precious of gifts.

一个可爱的女儿是生命中最珍贵的礼物。

7 January

All parents worry about all daughters at all times. The best cure is to hear them laughing.

父母无时无刻不在为爱女担忧。忧之深切，唯有女儿的笑声可解。

January 8

A very, very special daughter. Happiness beyond anything you ever thought possible.

你的女儿是独一无二的,她带来的快乐你永远想象不到。

January 9

Little daughter... She is so beautiful, so funny, so eager, so resolute. And she loves you with all her heart.

每一个女儿都是一个小天使,她美丽可爱,对世界充满热情;她坚毅果决,对父母有着毫无保留的爱意。

January 10

Having a daughter is like being involved in a perpetual treasure hunt – surprises at every turn!

养育女儿就像参加一场永无止境的寻宝游戏,你总能在意想不到的地方发现惊喜。

11 January

Small daughters give you hugs and sticky kisses and cry if they are scolded, and climb into your bed when they are frightened, and give you presents... and teach you how to love.

女儿会给你拥抱和甜甜的吻,会在挨训时掉眼泪,会在害怕时爬上你的床,会送你礼物……教会你如何去爱。

January 12

How small my world until you came along.

在你来临之前,我从未发现我的世界是这样狭小。

13 January

You dance for me, sing for me, travel the world for me.

你为我唱歌、跳舞,我通过你的眼睛环游世界。

January 14

Your daughter grows and there are unhoped-for gifts – successes, wisdom, new discoveries. Friendship. Laughter.

在女儿的成长之路上总能收获惊喜——你为她的成功而欢呼,因她的智慧而欣慰,你和她一起庆祝每一个新发现,分享每一份快乐,你是她成长的良伴。

15 January

When no one else understands, a daughter does.

即便你被整个世界误会,女儿总能理解你。

January 16

Thank you for bringing exclamation marks to our existence.

感谢你为我们的生活带来的所有惊喜。

17 January

Keep a little of this innocence, this clear, untarnished joy, this trust, this eagerness, whatever comes.

珍惜与女儿在一起的所有时光吧,哪怕是撷取一点童真的岁月珍藏在记忆里。享受她的信任,她的热切,她带给你的纯粹的快乐。

January 18

Where are you going, my girl? I cannot guess – only hope that it will all be wonderful. All I can promise is that I will do all I can do to make it so.

你要去向何方呢，我的女儿？我猜不到你的未来，只能祝你一切顺利。我将尽我所能，让你的旅途越发精彩，这便是我唯一能许下的承诺。

19 January

Looking back to the day you were born we smile. How could we begin to suspect the astonishments held in the bundle of blanket?

回想起你出生的那天，笑容就浮上我们的脸颊。这小小襁褓中的人儿将为我们带来多少惊喜和感动啊，又有谁会怀疑这一点呢?

January 20

Heads of petunias. Fluff-covered toffees. A lifetime of gifts. A lifetime of loving. But best of all, dearest, is knowing you're mine.

你像牵牛花一样可爱,像太妃糖一样甜美,你是生活给予的爱的礼物。最棒的是,你永远是属于我的。

21 January

A thank-you to my daughter. For seeing to it that my life is never dull, for keeping me on my toes.

感谢你,我的女儿,我的人生因你而精彩。

January 22

Brave, kind, loving – that's my girl. Special. Wonderful.

勇敢、善良、美好、独一无二——这就是我的女儿。

23 January

Daughters – keep us going well after our sell-by date.

当我们年华不再,女儿就是支撑我们走下去的动力。

January 24

We have a daughter, and are baffled from the very first, as she grows and changes by the minute. Utterly herself. Most dear of all possessions – yet never totally possessed.

我们有一个女儿。起初,她的成长和变化是那样迅速,让我们有些不知所措。这样一个独立的灵魂,是我们最珍贵的所有,可是也从未完全拥有过。

25 January

Daughter every single day you astonish or delight me – and often both.

我的女儿，因为你的到来，惊喜和赞叹交织着充满了我的每一天。

January 26

Loved you the second I saw you. Love you all the more with each passing year.

我爱你，从看到你的那一刻起；我爱你，历久弥深，不因岁月流逝而消减。

27 January

A daughter's good news brightens my drabbest day.

女儿的好消息照亮了我最灰暗的日子。

January 28

Thank you for wilting dandelions, for twigs of blossom, for wet pebbles, for fluff-covered toffees, for sticky kisses. Thank you for loving me.

感谢你给我采摘的蒲公英,结满花苞的枝条,沾着水珠的鹅卵石,松软的太妃糖和湿漉漉的吻。最感谢的,是你对我的爱。

29 January

Do it all, my love! Fly. Swim. Sail. Climb. Dance. Sing. You've only one lifetime. Start now if you want to fit it all in.

勇敢地去尝试吧,宝贝!去探寻天空、陆地和海洋,去攀登、跳舞和歌唱。从现在开始,跟随着你的心,去体验一切可能。

January 30

Dearest daughter. I wish you happy. Now and always.

最亲爱的女儿，我希望你永远快乐。

31 January

To have a daughter to us it is a miracle. Greatest of gifts. Dearest of daughters.

女儿,是生命的奇迹,是最好的礼物,是父母爱的归宿。

February

☼ ⛅ ☁ 🌧 💨 🌨

1 February

Thank you for all the unexpected phone calls, the envelopes stuffed with cuttings and drawings and dried leaves and photographs – and letters apparently written while riding a camel!

感谢你,我的女儿。为所有那些不期而至的来电,为那些装满了剪纸和图画、晒干的树叶和照片的信封,还有那些明显是骑在骆驼背上时写的信。

February 2

Thank you for your wonder at the world.

感谢你,为这个世界带来的所有神奇与美好。

3 February

There comes a day when a daughter becomes a friend.

有一天，你会发现，女儿成了你的知心朋友。

February 4

A small daughter looks at her mother and promises herself she will never act like that or speak like that or make such daft mistakes. But she will. She will.

小女孩看着她的妈妈,并暗自许诺,自己永远不会做那样的傻事,说那样的傻话和犯那样的错误。可这些承诺终究会落空。

February

5

A daughter reminds you of all the things you had forgotten about being young.

有了女儿，那些尘封已久的青春岁月会重新回到你的记忆里。

February 6

I wish you joy – success and friendship. Love. Wonder and discovery.

我希望你永远快乐,能品尝到成功的喜悦,收获珍贵的友情和爱情,永葆探索世界的热情。

7 February

Clear eyes, unblemished skin, and hair as soft as thistledown. A laugh that is all delight. A smile, all love. Your rounded arms stretched out to me. Your head nestled in my shoulder.

明亮的眼睛,无暇的肌肤,蓟花的冠毛一般柔软的秀发。你微笑着,带着满满的爱向我伸出双臂,枕在我的肩膀上休憩。

February 8

There you are, taller than I am, more streetwise than I am – and gentle too. Kind. Loving. More complex than I ever dreamed. And happy. I am proud of you.

你长大了,长得比我高了,比我更聪明,也更温柔了。你善良、有爱,比我想象的要成熟。你成为了一个快乐的人,我因你而骄傲。

February

Before a daughter has finally decided who she is and what she wants to be, her family are near bankrupt. Ice skates. Flute. Ballet shoes. Riding breeches. Paints. Theatrical make-up. Scuba gear. Microscope.

在女儿找到自己的人生方向，决定自己想要成为什么样的人之前，父母总濒临破产的边缘，买滑冰鞋、长笛、芭蕾舞鞋、马裤、绘画颜料、舞台化妆品、潜水镜、显微镜。

February 10

What do I most wish for you? A belief in the fundamental worth of humankind, and that, my dear, includes yourself.

我对你最深切的希望是什么呢？是希望你相信生而为人最本真的价值，也要相信你的价值。

11 February

You lighten my days and lift my spirits. In you I am young again.

你点亮了我的每一天,唤起我的热情。有你在身边,我得以重返青春。

February 12

Daughters rarely do the things you dread. They choose the things you never bargained for.

女儿们很少会做让你担心的事情,但她们的一些选择往往让你始料未及。

13 February

Daughters do wonderful things, astonishing things, better than you ever dreamed.

每一个女儿，都会给父母带来连做梦也想不到的惊喜。

February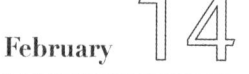

Here you are, my lovely daughter. Safe and sound. Welcome and wonderful. In no way like anyone else.

可爱的女儿,你在我的身边,我感到安全又温暖。你是那样的美好,是我的唯一。

15 February

You change and you grow – but are forever my dearest daughter.

不论你经历多少成长和改变,你永远都是我最亲爱的女儿。

February 16

We are so proud of all you have become.　　你成长中的一切都让我们感到骄傲。

17 February

Dear daughter. I hope that when you are very, very old you can look back and say "Heavens. That was a lovely life."

亲爱的女儿,我希望你能在白发苍苍的时候回顾人生,然后由衷地感叹:"我度过了多么美好的一生啊!"

February 18

A daughter's clothes can be very silly indeed. As silly as yours were at the same age. Just differently silly.

你也许会觉得女儿的衣着怪异,傻里傻气,但你当年也是这样。母女两代人,年少时都一样。

19 February

But I held you close and showed you sunlight, leaf shadows, yellow daisies – and you smiled and began to discover wonder.

我将你抱入怀中，带你去看明亮的阳光、树叶的阴影和黄色的雏菊。你笑了，然后开始发现世界的美好。

February 20

Thank you for seeing to it that my life never gets monotonous. Extraordinary decisions. Extraordinary adventures. Et voila!!

感谢你让我的生活变得如此丰富多彩：和你一起做出的每一个决定，和你一起经历的每一段旅程，都意义非凡。这样的生活太棒了！

21 February

This was the best time. But, then. So was the day of your birth, the day you recognized me, the day you first sat up. Each day has been the best.

这是我生命中最棒的一天了。啊,不对,你出生的那天,认出我的那天,第一次学会坐起来的那天,都是我生命中最棒的时刻!

February 22

Memories have linked our lives so often and so long that we are almost one. I am myself – and you are totally unique. Yet we are linked forever. By experience. By love.

生活中，共同的回忆拉近我们的距离，我们仿佛早已不分彼此，但又是两个完全独立的个体，生命紧紧交织是因为相同的经历和浓烈的爱意。

23 February

How fast time spins another generation – child giving way to child – joy to joy.

光阴荏苒,弹指一挥间,生命的接力棒已经传给了下一代,父母与子女,角色总随时间变换,永远不变的,是那份拥有爱的喜悦。

February 24

Thank you for the train rides and the roller-coasters. Thank you for running with me in the rain. And sprawling with me in the summer sun.

感谢你,我的女儿。感谢你陪我乘坐火车,玩过山车,与我一起在雨中奔跑,一同拥抱夏日的艳阳。

25 February

Each day brings new surprises, new delights. And with them anxieties... never known before.

和你在一起的每一天都有新的惊喜和欢乐,可快乐的背后也藏着我对你的忧虑,只是我从未表露而已。

February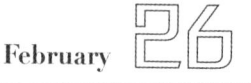

When you were small we tried to stand between you and sorrow. And now, when we are old, you have taken on that role and with loving hearts fend off the years and take the weight of our anxieties.

在你小时候,我们帮你扫除所有的悲伤,现在我们已经年老,你勇敢地站起来,带着一颗充满爱的心,直面人生的悲喜,帮我们减轻忧虑。

27 February

A daughter may want to follow in your footsteps. Or climb Everest.

女儿的未来或许会跟随你的脚步,或许会勇攀高峰,走向一片全新的天地。

February 28

Thank you for believing my birthday cakes were magical, my paintings amazing, my stories the best in the world…

感谢你，我的女儿，因为你相信我做的生日蛋糕有奇妙的魔力，因为你相信我的画作无可比拟，因为你相信我讲的故事世界上最有趣……

Daughter every single day you astonish or delight me – and often both.

我的女儿,因为你的到来,惊喜和赞叹交织着充满了我的每一天。

FOR MY DAUGHTER
女儿是父母的万花筒
365 Daily Messages of Love
❷

［英］帕姆·布朗 —— 著

新星出版社　NEW STAR PRESS

March

1 March

I worry about you. Whether you're happy or sad. If you have succeeded. If you have failed... Near or far away, that's what mothers do.

不论你是喜悦还是伤心,成功或是失败……不论你是在我身边还是远游在外,我都关心着你,因为你是我的女儿。

March

I live two lives. Mine and yours.

我的生活由两部分组成,那就是你的和我的。

  March

Everything comes in useful in the end. All the mistakes, all the pain, all the loss – just as much as the hard work and the learning and the love.

你所经历过的一切都会成为生命的财富。你犯过的错误，承受过的痛苦，经历过的失去和付出的努力，学到的知识和得到的爱一样意义非凡。

March 4

Your daughter. Your joy and your anxiety forever.

你的女儿,永远是你快乐的源泉,也永远是你操心的对象。

  March

When you were little you gave me forget-me-nots and daisies. Now you give me a world of wonder.

你小时候,会为我采摘勿忘我和小雏菊。现在你长大了,让我的生活每一天都充满了惊喜。

March

Light the blue touch-paper and stand well back. She may be a squib or a rocket. But wonderful!

点燃蓝色的导火纸,然后退后旁观,女儿的未来可能会像爆竹,猛然发出一声巨响,或像火箭,一飞冲天。但都无比美妙!

7 March

Dad has long and earnest conversations with his baby daughter. He tells her she is noisy, undisciplined and manipulative – and she will be sent back if she doesn't pull herself together. And the baby smiles complacently. She has him exactly where she wants him.

爸爸和她的小女儿进行了诚恳的长谈,爸爸说:"你整天哭闹,又不听话,还爱指使我们做这做那。如果你再不改正,就一定把你送回去。"小女儿露出得意的甜笑,反正她任何时候都能拿捏得住她的爸爸。

March 8

The happiest of wishes to our most astonishing delightful daughter... And thank you for the years of wonder that made you what you are.

致我们最可爱、最令人惊奇的女儿,我们希望你永远快乐。还要感谢这些美好的岁月,造就了美好的你。

9 March

No daughter decides to give up any hobby until her parents have bought all the required kit.

在父母买下所有需要的装备之前,没有一个女儿会放弃自己的任何一个爱好。

March 10

Wherever you are – in city street or in the hush and glimmer of a summer wood – our love is with you. It shines in the quiet pool. It wheels above you in the flight of geese.

无论你在哪里,我的女儿,是在城市的喧嚣中奔走,还是在夏日的丛林中漫步,我们的爱永远与你同在。它就藏在你经过的池塘里,在太阳下泛着柔光,或是在掠过天空的雁群里,在你的上空盘旋。

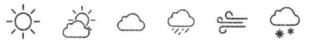

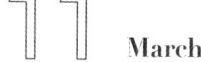

11 March

The older you get, the dearer you become.　　你越长大，就越贴心。

March 12

Just when you've settled to worrying about your teenage daughter, you suddenly realise the teenage years are passed – and she's fine!

只有当你已不再为青春期女儿担忧时,才会突然意识到,她的青春期已经悄然逝去——她一切安好!

13 March

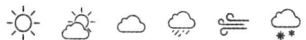

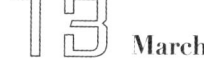

Your first swan. Your first day by the sea. Your first walk through a field of spring flowers. The first time you heard and loved Mozart. In sharing your childhood discoveries, I have relived my own.

你第一次见到天鹅，第一次去海边，第一次在开满鲜花的田野上漫步，第一次听莫扎特然后爱上了他的音乐。我分享着你童年许许多多的第一次，我也倍感欣慰。

March 14

You were a very lovely baby – but you've improved with every passing year.

你是那样的可爱,每一天,每一年,都比之前可爱一点点。

15 March

Mothers worry about their babies, their toddlers, their teenagers and do their best to keep them safe and happy. Even when they are grandmas. They can't help it.

从牙牙学语到蹒跚学步，再到青春懵懂，母亲对女儿的担忧从未停止，她们倾尽一切守护孩子平安快乐。即使母亲已经成为祖母，也不会改变。

March 16

Here's your writing on an envelope and the day is no longer dull.

看到信封上你的笔迹,平淡的生活瞬间明亮了起来。

17 March

Thank you for all the gifts. The lukewarm tea. The poems and the paintings. The plants. The flowerings of your heart and mind. A little of yourself.

感谢你给我的所有——冷热适中的茶水，作的小诗和画作，种的植物，还有你美丽的心灵和聪颖的大脑，以及你自己。

March 18

A blink of an eye, it seems, since you were beaming up at us from your cot or stomping unsteadily on the floor. And here you are – assured and independent, our most astonishing daughter.

致我无比优秀的女儿：你在婴儿床上冲我们笑的样子，在楼梯上摇摇晃晃向上爬的样子，仿佛还在昨天。但眨眼间，你长大了，变得自信和独立。

19 March

A daughter makes life worthwhile. 女儿让你的生活充满意义。

March 20

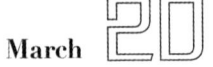

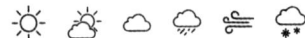

You see to it that I am never, never bored. 你将单调和寂寞永远赶出了我的生活。

21 March

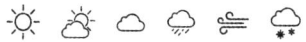

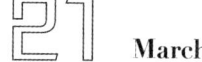

Thank you for those years of enchantment when you were very little – the rapturous, toothless smiles, the small perfections of your hands.

我的女儿，感谢所有有你陪伴的时光。我爱你小时候带来的所有惊喜，爱你咧着没牙的小嘴微笑，也爱你用小手创造出的完美奇迹。

March 22

The best thing you have given me is your friendship.

你给我最好的礼物就是你的友谊。

  **March**

I wish you all good things – especially the gift of being able to let go. Learn from sorrow and mistakes. Then go on.

我希望你拥有的一切都是美好的。尤其希望你能学会放下,懂得从悲伤和错误中学习,然后勇敢地走下去。

March 24

I have done little with my life, created nothing wonderful, given no new knowledge to the world. But I am content. I have given it a daughter. Most wonderful. Most wise.

我的一生都平凡无奇,既没有为世界带来什么伟大的创造,也没有贡献什么新知识。但我很满足,因为我养育了一个最优秀、最明智的女儿。

  March

A small child sits in the middle of the table and spreads her arms. And in that gesture gathers us to her heart. Her people, her loves, her world.

小女孩坐在桌子中间张开了双臂。那是她在呼唤所有爱的人,把亲人和世界都拥入怀中。

March 26

My daughter, my joy. From the moment I first saw you my life changed – and at times, I'll admit, I thought it for the worse! But how dull, how predictable life would have been without you.

我的女儿，我的快乐。第一眼看到你，我的生活就改变了。我必须坦白，有时我认为它变得更糟了。但是如果没有你，生活将会多么单调乏味啊！

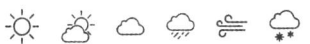

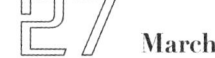

27 March

A daughter's triumph is a parent's triumph.　　女儿的成功就是父母的成功。

March 28

Every baby girl is utterly unique and gives a special sort of love.

每一个小女孩都是独一无二的,她们会给世界带来一份特别的爱。

  March

It's us against the world! We argue, disagree – and yet when the trouble comes we are together. Family!

即便是要与整个世界抗衡,我们也不是一个人。我们会争吵、有分歧,但当危机袭来我们总是共同应对。这,就是家人!

March 30

Parents try not to boast too blatantly about their daughter. But they can't help it.

父母在向别人炫耀女儿的时候会竭力让自己做得不要太露骨,可最后总是情不自禁。

  March

Daughters are liable to opt for wearing rags – or worse. To drop bombshells. They are trying lives on for size. The daughter you know and love is still there.

也许女儿的穿着会破破烂烂，甚至更糟；也许女儿会不时闯祸，给你带来坏消息，但这只是她探索世界、适应生活的方式，那个你了解并深深爱着的女儿，从未改变。

April

1 April

Daughters move away. To study, to travel, to marry. A thousand reasons. And yet they never leave – for they are a part of their families forever.

女儿总要离开父母,个中原因有成百上千,也许是为了求学,也许是为了旅行,也许是要嫁给心上人……但她们从未真正离开过,因为她们永远是家庭的一员。

April

To see one's daughter happy is happiness enough.

父母的满足和喜悦总是很简单,那就是看到自己的女儿开心。

Thank you for those mornings – just you and me in our dressing gowns, tea and toast and talk.

我深深感谢所有那些有你陪伴的早晨，我们穿着晨衣，一起品茶、碰杯和闲谈。

April 4

She appears not to listen to a word you say – but in a few years she'll be quoting you to her children as the font of wisdom.

也许女儿现在听不进你的说教,但假以时日她会明白这些至理名言,并把你的话原封不动地讲给她的孩子听。

5 April

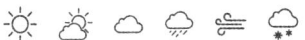

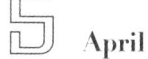

A daughter's smile delights the heart.

女儿的笑容点亮心灵。

April 6

I know you. I know your courage and good sense. I know that you will build a good and happy life. For yourself – and all about you.

我了解你,我相信你的勇气和判断力,我相信你会努力构建一个幸福美好的未来。为你自己,也为所有关心你的人。

7 April

"Welcome to the world" we said – in awe of your smallness, the exquisite detail of your tiny hands. The possibilities. Not knowing the astonishments that you held inside yourself, waiting to bewilder and delight us.

"欢迎你来到这个世界！"在你出生时，我们如是欢呼，我们惊叹于你精巧细腻的小手，畅想着你会拥有无限可能。那时，我们还不知道，小小的你在未来会为我们带来多少惊奇，让我们不知所措，也让我们欣喜。

April

Daughters are more precious than gold.
More precious than any inanimate thing,
however beautiful.

女儿比黄金更珍贵。没有生命的东西，再怎样美丽，也不及女儿的万分之一。

  April

The day a mother finds the perfect, right size, almost new pair of boots in the sales – is the day her daughter decides to give up roller-skating.

母亲发现一双漂亮时髦、尺码合适的打折轮滑鞋的那一天,往往就是女儿决定放弃学轮滑的日子。

April 10

Ride with me, straight and beautiful; ride beside me. Behind us lies the gentle country, the patches where you stumbled. Before us lies land stretching to a wide horizon – your world to discover and explore.

我们一起骑行,你熟练地跟在我身边。在我们身后,是我们可爱的家乡,你曾在那片田野上奔跑。在我们眼前,宽阔的道路铺展开来,一直延伸到远处的地平线。那里是你的未来,是等着你探索的世界。

11 April

I wish you joy in the great things of life – but also in the little things. A flower, a bird, the friendship of a cat.

女儿，我希望你既能为巨大成就而欢呼，也能为生活中的小确幸而欣喜，比如为一朵花，为一只小鸟，抑或是和一只猫建立友谊。

April 12

Dear daughter. Be a wife, a nun, an engine driver, a nurse, an architect, a lady in a shoe shop. Be what you want to be. What you need to be. I'll back you all the way.

亲爱的女儿，做你想做的事，去成为你想成为的人吧。无论你未来的角色是妻子、修女、司机、护士、建筑师还是鞋店售货员，我永远是你坚实的后盾。

13 April

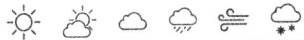

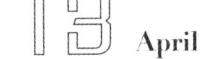

We feel with her – each restlessness, each fear, each pain. She laughs and we are overjoyed.

我们担忧着她的担忧，恐惧着她的恐惧，痛苦着她的痛苦。但只要女儿一笑，我们就无比欢喜。

April 14

A daughter is your excuse for playing with dolls again.

有了女儿,大人就有借口玩洋娃娃啦。

  April

Mothers do a lot of worrying about their daughters – however capable and sensible they are. It goes with the territory.

无论女儿有多精明强干,母亲总是为女儿操碎了心。这是亲情使然,再自然不过。

April 16

Thank you, my dearest girl, for emails, gifts and letters that are exactly right. Thank you for giving me advice. Thank you for letting me into your life.

感谢你,我最亲爱的女儿,你发来的每一封邮件,送的每一份礼物和书信都在我最需要的时候温暖了我的心。感谢你给我的建议,感谢你让我走进你的生命。

17 April

Daughters can break your heart and mend it. Almost simultaneously.

即便女儿伤了你的心,她也能立刻将它修补好。

 April 18

We've learned over years patience and understanding, loss and forgiveness.

随着时光流逝,我们最终学会了耐心和理解,失去与原谅。

19 April

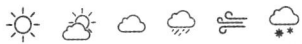

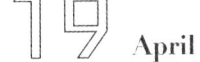

Daughters, in their hour of triumph, catch your eye and grin.

女儿在欢呼胜利的瞬间，总能捕捉到父母洋溢着骄傲的笑眼。

April 20

Life is never dull with a daughter.　　　　有了女儿，生活永远不会无趣。

 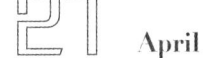 April

Small threads bind parents and daughters together in love and understanding.

爱与理解是连接父母与女儿的细线。

April 22

Daughters grow, change and weave most unexpected lives. But still the wonder grows – for in the alteration love persists.

女儿总会成长、改变,编织最意想不到的人生。纵使她给你的惊喜总在变化,但对你的爱却始终不变。

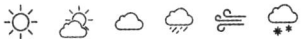

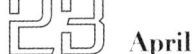

23 April

You have brought a sparkle to my life.   你点亮了我的生命。

April

Thank you for giving me back stars and fallen leaves, winter beaches, summer woods.

感谢你，我的女儿。因为你，我开始欣赏浩瀚的星空，观赏秋日的落叶，享受冬日的沙滩，赞叹夏日的森林。

  April

Dearest daughter – we were wonderstruck when we first saw your face, first held your tiny hands. We did not know that moment was only the beginning of wonders.

亲爱的女儿,第一次看到你的脸、握住你的小手时,我们都惊喜极了。那时我们还不知道,这一切只是奇迹的开始。

April 26

You have given my life a greater meaning.　　你赋予了我的生活更深远的意义。

  April

When no one can get through to anyone by phone or e-mail there are daughters in the house.

当你用电话或是电子邮件跟谁都联系不上时,幸好家里还有女儿在。

April

It's nice to have a daughter to hand to plot parties.

对于家庭中互有矛盾的成员来说,有个女儿在其中斡旋真是再好不过了。

Sometimes you just need someone to quietly hold you – and daughters know when.

有时候,你只是需要一个人轻轻地抱住你,而女儿总是在这个时候出现。

April 30

How can life ever be lonely while we share the planet?

有你和我待在同一个星球上,生活怎么会孤单呢?

A daughter is a book with a surprise on every page.

女儿就像一本书,打开之后,每一页都有惊喜。

★ FOR MY DAUGHTER ★
女儿是父母的万花筒
365 Daily Messages of Love
③

[英]帕姆·布朗 —— 著

新星出版社　NEW STAR PRESS

May

1 May

Dear girl, I wish that I could take your troubles and bury them so deep that they could never surface. I can't. But I am always here to share them and help as best I can to set things right.

亲爱的女儿，多么希望我可以将你的坎坷带走，再把它们深深埋藏，这样你就永远不必为此悲伤。但我不能，不过我会永远在你身边，分担你的悲伤，尽我所能帮助你走出阴霾。

May 2

Child. Clear crystal. Bright and clear faceted as none before you. Catching the light from every lovely thing and turning it to rainbow.

孩子的心像水晶一般明澈。那独一无二的切面，捕捉着每一道爱的光芒，将其变成一道彩虹。

3 May

Thank you for sharing things with me. Bars of chocolate. Cupcakes. Secrets.

感谢你和我分享的一切——巧克力、杯子蛋糕还有小秘密。

May 4

How very small you were. The things I wished for you seemed too large and ponderous for such a little creature. So I gave you my finger to hold and a kiss to welcome you into the world.

你出生时,是那么小的一个人儿,我想要给你的东西对你来说似乎太大太重,所以我伸出手来拥抱你,轻轻地亲吻你,欢迎你的到来。

5 May

You are now utterly independent and yet. I still share your joys and your successes and your sorrows.

如今的你已经完全独立,但我依然在你身边,分享着你的喜悦、成功和悲伤。

May 6

Until you have a daughter you don't realise how dull your life has been.

有了女儿才会知道你之前的生活有多么单调。

7 May

Mothers are proud of their grown-up daughters – but still hoard every memento of their childhood.

母亲为已经长大成人的女儿感到骄傲，但仍然珍藏着她们童年的每一件纪念品。

May 8

All disappointments, all failures fade like mist before this golden girl. Our daughter.

所有的失望和所有失败的痛苦都像迷雾一般消散。因为我的女儿出生了。

May 9

A small daughter's life is beset with the need to possess, to them, most necessary gear. Flat shoes and block shoes, deck shoes and trainers. A recorder and oboe. A guitar. A bike.

小女孩的生活总是需要各种各样的必备品。有平底鞋和绑带鞋,有帆布鞋和运动鞋。还有吉他和双簧管、录音机和自行车。

May 10

Like all past parents, I send you on your way, confident in all you are and all you will become. This is your time. Delight in all it brings. Things beyond imagination.

像天下所有父母一样,我送你踏上旅途,我相信你的实力,你一定会走出一条辉煌的路。这是你的时代,拥抱它所带来的一切吧,那将是一个你想象不到的世界。

11 May

Thank you for the years of wonder that made you what you are.

感谢这些美好的岁月造就了美好的你。

May 12

Dear daughter. Life has given you great power. The ancients knew it. Your strength outlasts all tyrannies, all loss and sorrow, all changes and all bigotries. You weave the world. You know the heart of things.

亲爱的女儿,生活赋予了你强大的力量。古人知道这种力量。你的力量能超越暴君的统治,能超越所有的失落与悲伤,能超越所有的动摇与偏执。你编织起世界,你洞悉了事物的核心。

13 May

A daughter is a book with a surprise on every page.

女儿就像一本书,打开之后,每一页都有惊喜。

May 14

Small daughters give their mothers appalling gifts – plaster and plastic, glitter and shine. Strange pots and stranger jewellery. And their mothers give them a pride of place and cherish them forever.

小女孩给妈妈的礼物总是稀奇古怪——灰泥、塑料和闪闪发光的东西,还有奇形怪状的锅子和首饰。母亲则给予了这些东西一片荣耀之地,永远地善加珍藏。

May 15

Daughters are difficult. Not every daughter perhaps. There may be some who have never flounced or stamped or pouted in their lives, never flung themselves flat or slammed doors hard behind them in their later life. There may be...

女儿们都很难弄。或许不是各个如此。比如有些孩子发起脾气来从不会上蹿下跳，噘嘴瞪眼，长大之后从不会气呼呼地往床上一躺或怒冲冲地摔门而去，再比如……

May 16

All parents have to learn to take messages and notes with equanimity... Bangkok. Been in local hospital but OK now. May go north at the end of the week. Not sure where to, but will let you know soon. P.S. Love to all!

面对孩子传来的每一条讯息,父母总要学会平静地接受,比如:我现在在曼谷;我在医院,但已经没事了;这周末要去北方,还没确定具体去哪里,但很快会告知你们。对了,我爱你们!

17 May

You came – and my life was changed forever.

你的到来永远改变了我的生活。

May 18

They are all kept safe, the birthday cards and Mother's Day cards and little gifts, just because you thought I'd like them. Tokens I have treasured since you were small. Amulets that heal my heart.

我珍藏着所有你送来的生日贺卡、母亲节贺卡和小礼物。因为你觉得我会喜欢它们。这是从你们小时候起我就倍加珍视的亲情的象征。它们是我深藏于心中的护身符。

19 May

Daughters come in every shape and size and disposition. But you're the one for me.

女儿们来到世界时身材和性格各不相同，但对我来讲，你们都是独一无二的。

May 20

Daughters spring surprises – it's part of their nature.

女儿们会带来惊喜,这是她们天性的一部分。

21 May

My dearest girl, you were a lovely baby, a fascinating child but look at you now! A marvel!

我最亲爱的女儿,你从一个可爱的婴儿成长为一个优秀的孩子,现在的你简直是一个奇迹!

May 22

Did I ever tell you how proud I am of you, or what delight you've given me? No? Then know it now. Hold it in your heart.

我有没有告诉你,我为你而骄傲,为你带来的所有欢乐感到自豪呢?没有吗?没关系,你现在知道了,请永远记在心中吧!

23 May

Dear daughter, hold in your heart the joys and sorrows of your childhood, so that you can understand those of your children.

亲爱的女儿,把你童年的快乐和悲伤都记在心中吧!这样当你为人母时,就能理解自己的孩子了。

May 24

Dear daughter, may you do something that you are proud of – even if it is very small.

亲爱的女儿，愿你做出令自己感到骄傲的事情，即便只是非常小的事。

25 May

Thank you for turning up when life had become monotonous.

感谢你的出现，改变了我单调乏味的生活。

May 26

Dearest daughter, thank you for being exactly what you are.

最亲爱的女儿,感谢你,做最珍贵的自己。

27 May

Having daughters is the best investment you will ever make against becoming bored.

养育女儿是你避免生活乏味的最佳投资。

May 28

Daughters like to astonish their parents – by showing abilities they never suspected. A gift for mathematics. Cooking. Gardening. Or flying aeroplanes. Perfect pitch. Or surgery.

女儿总能用各种意想不到的才能为父母带来惊喜。比如展示数学天赋,做出美味的饭菜,打理庭院;再比如驾驶飞行器,一展美丽的歌喉,或在手术室中救死扶伤。

29 May

In you I am young again.   在你身上,我重新找回了年轻的感觉。

May 30

I've watched you grow – and my love has grown with you.

看着你一天天长大,我对你的爱也与日俱增。

31 May

Thank you for making every day a new adventure.

感谢你,我的女儿,自从有了你,每一天都是新的冒险。

June

1 June

As you grow older I find more and more in you to astonish and delight me. How on earth did I manage to produce such a daughter?

随着你不断成长,我发现你越来越令我惊讶和快乐。拥有如此出色的女儿,我何其有幸啊!

June 2

Your first mayfly. Your first rainbow. Your first dinosaur. Thank you for the chance to rediscover the world.

你笔下的第一只蜉蝣、第一条彩虹和第一只恐龙都让我惊喜不已。感谢你,给了我重新认识世界的机会。

3 June

Daughters and mothers allow each other to fall off their respective diets – just once in a while.

女儿和母亲会容许对方悄悄抛开减肥计划,偶尔放飞一下。

June 4

A daughter who travels knows that she's fine. And has no notion that her mother and father don't know that fact and are out of their minds with worry.

女儿出去旅行时感觉自己一切都好。但她们不知道她们的父母并不知晓这个事实,总在魂不守舍地替她们担心。

5 June

I have so many memories of you, I have filed them away, wrapped in tissue, tied with silver thread, safe in the secret places of my mind.

我们之间留下了许许多多的回忆。我将它们小心归类，用银线精心包裹，珍藏在我记忆深处。

June

With the birth of a daughter one embarks on a lifetime's adventure.

女儿的出生标志着母亲开启了一场终生探险。

7 June

We two most ordinary people produced a marvel. You opened your eyes, looked at us and we knew you were already your own person – and a small shiver of wonder ran through us.

我们是一对再平凡不过的夫妻，但我们创造了奇迹，那就是我们的女儿。从你睁开眼睛，看向我们的那一刻起我们就明白，你是一个完全独立的生命——一种创造了奇迹的战栗传遍了我们全身。

June 8

We have to let go their hands. But the joys we knew before, remembered, are part of us all forever.

我们最终要放手。但我们之间所有的快乐时光，都会被永远藏在心里，成为我们生命的一部分。

9 June

My beautiful, clever, warm-hearted daughter... I try not to crow about you. But I can't help looking a little smug.

我的女儿，你是那样美丽、聪颖和善良。我竭力遏制住自己逢人便夸的冲动，但还是免不了有些沾沾自喜。

June 10

We showed you our world, but now you lead us into one we never knew.

我们带着你走进我们已经熟知的世界,但你却带着我们走向了一个充满未知的新奇之地。

11 June

Her days are as precious as mine were. They always will be. Our children make their own wonders.

我的青春时光珍贵易逝,女儿的亦然。女儿是我永远的珍宝,他们总在创造属于自己的奇迹。

June 12

Mothers dream of daughters, before they come, who will be academics, engineers, architects, artists, dancers, doctors, operatic singers. They get scruffs who climb trees. Rodeo riders. Bank clerks. Train drivers.

女儿出生之前,母亲总会憧憬女儿将来会做什么,她会成为学者、工程师、建筑师、艺术家或是舞者、医生、歌剧演员;她会因爬树而弄得一身邋遢;她也可能会成为骑手、银行家、火车司机。

13 June

However important a daughter becomes, however beautiful, however famous, to her mother she is utterly unchanged.

无论女儿如何变化,变得多么重要,多么美丽,拥有何等名望,在母亲的眼里,女儿永远都是她最爱的那副模样。

June 14

Thank you for having given me the chance to make mud pies again, to paddle in the sea, to sail a toy boat – to ride the fairground horses. Thank you for bringing back fun to all our lives.

感谢你,我的女儿,在你身边,我又有了机会玩泥巴,在海中踩水,将玩具小船送向远方,在游乐场骑木马。你将童真的快乐重新带回了我们的生活。

15 June

How can I call you mine – when you belong to yourself and to the world? And yet, we are linked together by love and memory and so belong to one another.

你属于你自己，属于这个世界，我又怎能将你据为己有呢？但是我们有共同的爱和回忆，我们的生命因此而连结，所以我们也是属于彼此的啊。

June 16

There is nothing, absolutely nothing that can cheer up a dismal evening of TV repeats and yesterday's leftovers more successfully than a message from a daughter.

沉闷的夜晚,吃着昨天的剩饭剩菜,看着电视里重播的节目,一切都让人提不起任何兴致,除非能收到一条来自女儿的消息。

17 June

Do you remember spring walks? Walking by a shining sea and the sound of gulls? I do, I do.

还记得那些春日里的漫步吗？那时，我们走在海边，看着海水在阳光下闪着波光，听着海鸥的阵阵鸣叫。记得，记得，我都还记得。

June 18

There's one thing about daughters. You're never sure who is going to step out of the chaos they call their room.

女儿总是这样,你永远都不知道当她们从乱糟糟的房间里走出来时会变成什么样。

19 June

I wish you discoveries and marvels.

我希望你每刻都有小惊喜,每天都有新发现。

June 20

I am rediscovering the world in you.
Seeing all things as if for the first time.

在你身上，我重新认识了这个世界。我眼中的一切，仿佛都是初次看到。

21 June

Daughters are so delightful one is tempted to freeze-dry them when they are small – first teeth, first steps, first words – unflawed forever. But their glory is in their infinite capacity for change.

总是想要将女儿的童年时代永远保存，因为她是那样可爱，第一颗乳牙，第一次走路，第一句话，永远那么纯洁无瑕。不过她们真正的闪光之处更在于成长中拥有无限可能。

June 22

If I had the power to make one wish for you, I would find it very hard to decide what gift to give you – what gift would help you to happiness. But in the end, I am certain that I would have chosen the best gift of all – and that is courage.

如果我能替你许一个愿，我会为该给你怎样的礼物而为难，什么礼物能给你带来幸福？但最终，我拿定了主意，要把最好的礼物送给你——那就是勇气。

23 June

I wish I could take all your troubles and wash them away, hang out your days to blow in the sunshine. Iron them and give them back to you all fresh and sweet and good as new.

真希望能把你所有的烦恼都洗去，把没有了烦恼的日子放在阳光下晾干、熨平，再交还到你的手里，那么新鲜、芬芳，像崭新的日子般美好。

June 24

A parent lives the suffering of a daughter – made worse by her inability to take it from her.

母亲对于女儿的痛苦感同身受,但却无法替女儿承担痛苦,这让母亲备受煎熬。

25 June

It's good when a mother or father and their daughter think of one another – store things in their minds to tell each other. People they've met, things they've done, astonishments, delights.

父母和女儿若是相互惦记着,把事情存在脑子里,留待见面时好好说上一番,这是一件多么美好的事啊!说说各自遇到的人,各自做过的事,那些稀奇的、让人高兴的东西。

June 26

Daughters like you are boxes of delight.　　女儿，你就像是装满了惊喜的魔法宝盒。

27 June

Daughters are sugar and spice – with a touch of Tabasco.

养育女儿总要尝遍多种滋味，有甜蜜，有香辛，还有一点点辣椒的刺激。

June 28

Thank you for every letter, every note you've ever sent to me. I have them all!

感谢你,我的女儿,你的每一封来信,每一张便条,我可都留着哪!

29 June

Daughters are more precious than one's dreams.

所有的梦想都比不上女儿珍贵！

June 30

As long as you love me, my dearest daughter, I'm OK.

只要你爱我,我最亲爱的女儿。我便一切安好。

You change and you grow – but are forever my dearest daughter.

不论你经历多少成长和改变,你永远都是我最亲爱的女儿。

★ FOR MY DAUGHTER ★

女儿是父母的万花筒

365 Daily Messages of Love

[英] 帕姆·布朗 —— 著

新星出版社　NEW STAR PRESS

July

1 July

A daughter often has the courage to do the things you didn't dare.

女儿往往有勇气去做你不敢做的事。

July 2

Dearest daughter. Most puzzling, most exciting and most loved.

我最亲爱的女儿,你是世界上最令人束手无策,最令人激动,又最招人疼爱的宝贝啦!

  July

How good it is, to reach the cafe, find a table, a cup of tea, a quiet meal, a review of the day's small triumphs. My daughter and my dearest friend.

走到咖啡馆,找到一张桌子,品一杯茶,静静地享用晚餐,回顾这一天小小的成就。我的女儿,我最亲爱的朋友。

July 4

Wave your daughter off to university or Canada and even as you dab your eyes rejoice in her freedom and courage.

女儿即将启程,前往外地上大学或是去加拿大。与她挥手作别,尽管湿了眼眶,但看到女儿无拘无束、勇往直前,也甚是欣慰。

  July

We were linked together by light, invisible chains – stronger than steel and indestructible.

我们之间的爱，就像一条无形的链子将我们紧紧相连——坚如钢铁，坚不可摧。

July 6

I saw such splendid things, listened to such wonders, and now your turn has come. The world is waiting for you, and the stars.

我见过无与伦比的美丽,听过绝妙的天籁之音。现在轮到你了,这个世界等待你去体验,浩瀚星空等待你去探索。

7 July

Thank you for giving me the joys of childhood all over again.

感谢你,让我仿佛回到小时候,重温儿时的快乐。

July 8

Each and every daughter brings a different gift.

每个女儿,都会带来不一样的惊喜。

  July

Dear daughter – explore the bits of the world I never got to, read the books I never read.

亲爱的女儿，去探索这世界上我从未踏过的土地，去阅读那些我从未看过的书。

July 10

Now you are moving on to new adventures, new loves, new friends but always, still, a part of us.

现在你踏上了新的冒险之旅,接触到了新的爱人和朋友,但是,我们总在你身边。

11 July

How could I manage without you? Near or far from me you give me hope and happiness.

没有你,我该怎么办? 无论你身在何处,你都给予我希望和幸福。

July 12

Daughters borrow things. But give you their love in payment.

女儿们会问你借这借那。但会用满满的爱来回报你。

13 July

A daughter's happiness lights up a mother's heart – even if that "child" is forty years old.

女儿的幸福，总会点亮妈妈的心——即使那个"孩子"已经 40 岁啦。

July 14

I watch you grow and change, a constant surprise, a constant wonder.

我眼见着你一天天长大,一点点变化。
你不断带给我惊奇,令我喜出望外。

15 July

Every year makes you more dear. Dear daughter – what did I do to deserve you?

一年一年,我对你的爱只会更多一点。亲爱的女儿——我何德何能,让你降临到我身边?

July 16

Sometimes I come across a bit of paper in your handwriting. A list. A thank-you. And you're there in the room. You always will be.

有时我不经意间看到几张纸,上面是你的笔迹。一张清单,一句感谢。这给我一种感觉,像你就静静地待在屋子里,一直在我身边。

17 July

A daughter grows from a little loving child into a dear companion.

女儿慢慢长大。从一个惹人爱的小女孩成长为我最亲密的伙伴。

July 18

A daughter is a member of a self-perpetuating species. Each only fully understands why their mothers shrieked and tore their hair out when their own daughter hits the Teens.

这件事情是循环往复的：只有当自己的女儿进入青春期开始叛逆的时候，她们才明白当初自己的母亲会大声尖叫，气得焦躁不安。

19 July

When I first saw you, you were charming. But with every year you have grown until you are no longer merely charming. You are magnificent. As a proud parent, I think you're "best in show".

我第一眼见到你的时候,你真是美极了。但看着你一年年长大,你已经不仅仅是美的化身了。你是无与伦比的珍宝。我为你而骄傲,你永远是我的"全场最佳"。

July 20

I watched over you, fed you, protected you. Be brave. Take possession of this sun bright air.

我的目光始终落在你身上,慢慢把你养大,又时刻保护着你。勇敢些,尽情沐浴这明媚的阳光吧!

July 21

Take courage, my lovely lass. Whatever you do – do it well. We are all behind you.

勇往直前吧,我亲爱的姑娘!无论你做什么——尽心尽力把它做好。我们是你坚强的后盾。

July 22

A daughter is the person you thought you would stop worrying about when she hits twenty-one. But who is still worrying you silly at forty-five.

你本以为女儿到了 21 岁,就不用再发愁她的事情了。但就算她到了 45 岁,还是会让你有操不完的心。

I will remember the first time I saw you and hold it in my heart forever.

我永远记得你降临到我身边的那一刻,那美好的瞬间将永远存放在我心头。

July 24

Dear, small, wide-eyed little daughter, I'll hold your shadow in my arms forever, even when you're grown.

亲爱的女儿，我的小宝贝，大大的眼睛一闪一闪，即便你长大成人了，我也会永远把你的影子拥在怀中。

  July

You are our gift to the future. With you the world is given new opportunities, new vision. In you lies hope.

你是我们赋予未来的礼物。有了你,世界便有了新的机遇、新的视野。你的到来带来了希望。

July 26

I have other joys – but the very best is you.　　所有的快乐都不及你带给我的幸福。

27 July

Some people seem to manage without a daughter. They don't know what they're missing.

有些人没有女儿,似乎日子也能过。但他们并不知道,自己错过了多少幸福。

July 28

Now you bring me books and useful things you pick up at the sales. Best daughter in the world.

现在,你会送我超划算的大减价书刊和各种实用的物品。你真是世界上最棒的女儿啦。

  July

I wish I could save you from anxiety and sorrow…

我希望我可以帮你拦下所有的焦虑和悲伤……

July 30

Parents may sigh to see their baby grow into a schoolchild, a schoolchild into an undergraduate, an undergraduate into a professional – with a life and loves all her own. But they love her exactly the same.

看着自己的孩子不断成长——咿呀学语的宝贝迈入小学,从小学到大学毕业,毕业后又开始职业生涯,拥有自己的生活,热爱自己的一切,父母可能会禁不住叹息。但他们给予孩子的爱从未改变。

  July

Thank you for making our lives so incredibly eventful.　　感谢你，让我们的生命无比绚丽与精彩。

August

1 August

A wise parent never promises anything till they've checked the bank balance.

聪明的父母从不会在查看银行账户之前就许下任何承诺。

August 2

Sometimes I wish I had treasures to pass on to you. But I gave what I could – your five bright senses, the world about you.

有时我真希望自己有什么宝贝能流传给你。但我给了我能拿出的一切——你用来感受外界的五官,以及我对你全部的爱。

August 3

So little time ago I took you to a cafe for a currant bun. And now you are escorting me into an astoundingly posh place for dinner. But still my girl.

不久前还是我带着你，到一个咖啡馆买葡萄干面包。转眼间，便是你陪着我，在金碧辉煌的地方享用晚餐。但你依然是我的好女儿，这一点永远不变。

August 4

Daughters set out on holiday to one destination – but e-mail you from somewhere completely different. Generally remote and a trifle dangerous.

假期里，女儿往往启程前往一个目的地，却从另一个地方给你发邮件。基本上都是很远，还有点儿危险的地方。

You walked and talked and we were enchanted. But all the time you were turning from our dream into your own reality.

你边走边说,我们听得如痴如醉。但是你如终在我们的梦中和你的现实世界中转换。

August 6

You are our bright star. You light our lives.   你是我们心中最亮的星,你照亮了我们的生命。

7 August

When you were born, you were an amazement a perfection, a wonder.

你降临的那一刻,真是令人惊喜万分,你完美得没有一丝瑕疵,像奇迹一般降临在我们面前。

August 8

I sleep more soundly when I know you're safe and well and happy.

当我知道你很安全、健康和幸福,我便睡得更安心了。

  August

Grow, my dearest daughter, learn and love. Skills you have never yet suspected can be yours. Explore, and find a place that's truly yours.

我最亲爱的女儿,快快成长吧,学习新的知识,也尝试着去爱。不要怀疑,你终将掌握那些尚未拥有的能力。去探索吧,找寻那个真正的自己。

August 10

From now on it is your journey. Good luck. Ride bravely. Ride well.

从现在开始,路是你自己的了。勇敢地踏上旅途。祝你好运。一路顺风。

11 August

No mother's hands ever forget her daughter's little bony hand clasped safe in hers on windy summer walks.

没有一个妈妈会忘记曾经女儿纤细的小手紧紧地牵住自己,两人一同在夏日有风的日子里漫步。

August 12

No job, no man, no opportunity is ever quite good enough for one's daughter.

没有什么工作、男人或者机会,是完全配得上自己女儿的。

You called today and the sun came out.　　你今天打来电话,我的世界都明亮了。

August 14

We field her as she falls. Wrap her against the cold. Boast casually to friends of her achievements. Hoard photographs in case we should forget.

她摔一跤,我们便赶忙抱住。气温下降,我们便给她裹得严严实实。我们不经意地向朋友炫耀她的成就,也会把她的照片珍藏起来,怕自己忘记这美好时光。

15 August

Every scrap of advice, every opinion, every suggestion, every piece of useful information that one gives a daughter vanishes like water into sand. Until, long after, a grown-up daughter gives her considered opinions upon some issue. And one recognizes it. Word for word.

我们给女儿的每一条建议,每一个想法,每一则有用的信息,如同渗入沙里的水,一去不复返。直到很久以后,已经长大成人的女儿面对某些事情,在深思熟虑后给出了她的观点,这时我们才欣喜地发现——每一个字都那么熟悉。

August 16

The telephone is a wonderful thing. It can offer a loving daughter a long distance shoulder to cry on.

电话真是太棒了!即使亲爱的女儿离得再远,她也可以有个肩膀,靠着哭泣。

17 August

We hold each other's hearts in keeping. 我们守护着彼此的心,永永远远。

August 18

With a daughter, life can never, never, never be monotonous.

有个女儿,生活永远不会枯燥乏味。

August 19

You think she'll be a rosebud – but be prepared. For a sunflower, an orchid or a daisy! Daughters are wonderful. But rarely what you expected.

你以为她是一朵含苞待放的玫瑰，但也不要太确定——她可能会成为向日葵、兰花或者雏菊！女儿是无与伦比的，但她往往会偏离你最初的期待。

August 20

Your daughter takes the paths you never found.

你的女儿选择的道路，是你从未走过的。

Every mother has drawers and boxes overflowing with everything her children ever wrote or drew or painted, stitched or made in woodwork. The passing years held like flies in amber.

每个妈妈都有几个抽屉和箱子，里面装满了孩子们所有写写画画的东西，还有亲手用木头制成的工艺品。这里面盛着似水流年，仿若一块凝固着飞虫的琥珀，稀世难寻。

August 22

If I could, I would spare you all the heart-sinking moments when happiness goes wrong.

如果可以，我愿分担你所有心碎的瞬间。当你的幸福迷失方向的时候，我会一直伴你左右。

  **August**

You were my new beginning. 你是我人生全新的开始。

August 24

My most precious gift – my dear lass.

我亲爱的姑娘——你是我最珍贵的礼物。

  August

Dear girl. You changed my life. Where I would be without you I just don't know. Not here. Not as happy as I am.

亲爱的女儿,你改变了我的生活。如果没有你,我真的不知道自己会在哪里。不会是现在这般模样,也不会如此幸福。

August 26

You are my greatest treasure – my dearest girl.

我最亲爱的女儿——你是我最珍贵的财富。

27 August

Daughters are given to making announcements. I've signed on to crew a boat to Singapore. I've invited my head teacher to dinner... Today. I'm leaving home. I'm going to be a nun. I'm having my hair dyed pink.

女儿总爱宣布消息。我签约成为了一名船员,和他们一同前往新加坡。我邀请了我的班主任共进晚餐……今天,我要离家出走,我要削发为尼,我要把头发染成粉色。

August 28

Some daughters give florists' bouquets, Cartier watches and Cointreau. Some daughters send shrubs, sweaters and home-made jam. The thing is – daughters know exactly what one needs.

有些女儿会送精心挑选的花束、卡地亚手表和君度美酒。有些女儿则送小灌木、毛衣和自制果酱。关键是，女儿们总是知道父母需要什么。

Dearest daughter – once I held you in my arms. Now you are grown and free. But I still hold you in my heart.

我最亲爱的女儿——曾经,我把你抱在怀中。现在,你已长大成人,过着自由的生活。但我一直牵挂着你。

August 30

Never forget – you're not just special to me. You're special. And that's that.

永远不要忘记——你不仅于我而言是特别的。你本来就与众不同。就是这样。

  August

Here's my daughter, the budding ballerina. In a pink tutu. On roller-skates.

这就是我的女儿,新生代芭蕾舞演员。穿着粉色小纱裙,脚踩小小轮滑鞋。

Mothers are proud of their grown-up daughters
but still hoard every memento
of their childhood.

母亲为已经长大成人的女儿感到骄傲，但仍然珍藏着她们童年的每一件纪念品。

★ FOR MY DAUGHTER ★

女儿是父母的万花筒

365 Daily Messages of Love

5

[英]帕姆·布朗 —— 著

新星出版社　NEW STAR PRESS

September

7 September

I wish you what I have wished you since your life began: May you never cease to search and challenge. May you discover what you want to do – and do it well.

自你降临到这世上,我对你的希冀便一直如此:愿你毕生坚持上下求索,勇于挑战。愿你发现你想做的事情,并做得精彩。

September

A child gives us our own first times, all over again.

孩子带我们回到自己的幼年时光,重新来过。

  September

Who brings me small surprises? Who makes me cups of tea? Who lets me watch my programme though she's dying to change channels? You my dearest daughter. A daughter in a million.

是谁带给我小小惊喜？是谁给我沏的茶？是谁心里巴不得赶快换频道，却还是让我看了想看的节目？是你啊，我最亲爱的女儿；百万人之中才得一个的好女儿。

September 4

Mothers watch their daughters toss themselves out of aircraft, or vanish into the depths of the sea, with a certain anxiety – but as they land, or emerge from the waves like happy seals – they rejoice. They could, by a trick of time, been born Victorians.

妈妈看着她们的女儿从万米高空一跃而下,或者潜入深海不见踪影,肯定会焦急难耐;但是看到女儿安全着陆,或者像快乐的海豹一样从海浪中探出头来,她们又变得欢欣雀跃。这样的妈妈,可真是活脱脱的维多利亚时代母亲的再现啊!

  September

Reach out to us and we are there. As you have always been for us.

把手伸向我们吧,我们一直在这里。你总是义无反顾地支持着我们,我们也会陪在你身旁。

September

I suppose the best thing I could wish you would be enthusiasm.

我觉得我可以给予你的最棒的祝福，便是愿你永葆热情。

7 September

Daughters are an excuse for us to indulge in the purchase of quantities of little pink and frilly garments and tiny, tiny shoes.

正是有了宝贝女儿,我们才会尽情享受购物的乐趣——数不尽的小小粉色百褶裙,还有不到巴掌大的小鞋子。

September 8

A lovely daughter, reflecting beauty back into the world. Making all things new.

可爱的女儿,你把美丽重新播撒给了世界,让万事万物都重获新生。

  September

A daughter can go through a ballet class like a sylph, like a swan, change into dungarees and head off for a game of tennis with the boys.

女儿就是百变精灵：一会儿是芭蕾舞课堂上的窈窕淑女，像天鹅一般优雅动人；一转身又换上工装裤，跟男孩子打网球去了。

September 10

Dear daughter, sometimes, things will go wrong. The secret is not to let them overwhelm you. Courage and hope will see you through.

亲爱的女儿，有时事情往往不如人所愿。秘诀就是不要让它们压得你喘不过气儿来。鼓起勇气，充满希望，你便会渡过难关。

11 September

She doesn't love you any more, she says. She scowls and turns away. But, moments later, here she is against your knee, her little arms about you, her sweet, soft face nuzzling your rib cage. A muffled, "love you". And the sun has come out again.

她说,她再也不爱你了。她当时怒发冲冠,然后转头离去。但是,过了一会儿,她又跑到你面前,小小的胳膊抱着你,可人儿软软的小脸蛋在你胸前蹭来蹭去。她含含糊糊地说:"爱你"。乌云散去,阳光再次撒入心田。

September 12

Even the best of parents know they are not owed anything. They are paid by all you give the world.

就算是世界上最棒的父母,也知道他们不欠任何东西。他们偿还的是你给世界的一切。

Parents droop a little sometimes – but then they think of their daughters – their verve and their good-heartedness, their achievements and their beauty. And feel much better.

有时父母会有点儿消沉。忽然,他们想起了自己的女儿——她们是那样充满活力,心地善良,成就非凡,还美丽动人,顿时就感觉好多啦。

September 14

Little girls grow up when you're not looking. 小女孩往往在不经意间就长大了。

September 15

There are things I cannot stick together, or heal with a hug... I wish I had some magic that could make such things come right. All I can do is be here. Always.

有些事情我无能为力，既不能实现破镜重圆，也不是一个拥抱便可以治愈……真希望我拥有魔法，让那些不幸都烟消云散。我能做的就是在你身旁，永远陪伴着你。

September 16

Thank you for giving me something to boast about!

谢谢你,让我有了引以为傲的资本!

17 September

How on earth did I produce so beautiful, so caring, so capable, so kind, so gifted a daughter? Thank you for coming into my life.

我怎么能诞下如此美丽动人，对人关怀备至，能力出众，善解人意又天赋异禀的好女儿呢！谢谢你，走进我的生命。

September 18

It's hard to accept that this tall, slender, beauty dressed entirely in a navy suit is the little girl who loved a frilly dress that swirled. And only a handful of years ago. But she's still crazy about peanut brittle!

这个身穿海军服的女孩,身材高挑、纤细苗条又美丽动人。真是难以置信,她小时候可是对百褶裙情有独钟,这才是几年之前的事情而已。但她仍然痴迷花生脆!

19 September

The jewel in my crown. My own dear girl.   皇冠上的绝世珠宝，我最亲爱的女儿。

September 20

You came and flung open a window to a wider world.

你来到这世界，仿佛猛然推开了一扇窗，呈现在眼前的，是更广阔的天地。

  September

A baby lies snug in its nutshell, so small, so delicate, so vulnerable. We feel inadequate to keep her safe, to see her through to womanhood. Not recognising the hidden strength that will set her growing, inch by inch, into a flowering tree.

小宝贝舒舒服服地躺在妈妈肚子里,她是那么弱小,那么柔软。我们好像没有足够的信心,让她安全长大,成长为美丽动人的女性。也未曾发现能够助她成长的秘密力量,她就这样一点点长大,成为了一棵开满花朵的大树。

September 22

Days of adventure. Days of despair. Down in the depths, up in the air. All my confusion suddenly clear – my gift to the future. My daughter. My dear.

细数那些惊险刺激的日子，绝望透顶的日子。人生大起大落，有时跌入深渊，有时直冲云霄。霎时间，我心中所有的迷乱都荡然无存——我的女儿，我最亲爱的人，你是我留给未来最美好的礼物。

  September

How fortunate I am to have a daughter like you. Someone to laugh with, share secrets, a reassurance in the darkest times. I look back on the happy times we've known – and wish you a year, a future, packed with delights.

我有你这样一个女儿,是多么幸运啊!可以有人一起开怀大笑,分享秘密,即使是最黑暗的日子也有你这颗定心丸。回顾我们经历的幸福时光——我祝愿你未来每一年,都充满了喜悦。

September

Daughters are like those small, attractive, unnamed seedlings that stun you by their sudden growth, and explosion into unexpected flower.

女儿就像那些迷人的无名小幼苗,她们会突然成长,令你大吃一惊,然后迸发力量,成为出乎你意料的美丽花朵。

  September

A daughter can be guaranteed to do the unexpected, it's what keeps life interesting.

女儿肯定会做出你始料未及的事情,生活岂不正是因此而有趣。

September 26

Thank you for giving me back young eyes and a young heart.

谢谢你,让我重新拥有一双年轻的眼睛和一颗年轻的心。

  September

Daughters are daft. It's expected in their teens, but they don't improve with age. Walk out of university. Climb Everest. Marry impossible men. Their lives are rarely dull. Just constant sources of anxiety.

女儿们好傻啊!早知她们十几岁的时候会犯傻,但是随着年龄增长,情况并未有所好转。大学毕业,攀登珠穆朗玛峰,嫁给不可忍受的男人。她们的生活很少会平淡。一想到她们呀,就让人操心得不行。

September 28

There are daughters who give you lumpy parcels tied with string and there are daughters who give you gift-wrapped boxes elegant with flowers and bows and curly ribbons, but the contents are the same – affection under various guises.

有些女儿送的礼物包装粗糙，外面随便用绳子捆 捆。有些女儿则把礼物装在专门的礼盒中，再点缀上鲜花、蝴蝶结和卷曲的缎带，看着十分精美。但无论哪种包装，里面的内容都是一样的——对你满满的爱。

  September

Dear daughter – you have shown yourself to be wise and good and kindly and loving. As in our hearts we always knew you would.

亲爱的女儿——你是个聪明伶俐、心地善良、温柔体贴并且惹人喜爱的小姑娘。在我们心中,早就知道你会成为如此出色的人了。

September

No one deserves to be loved as a daughter loves – it is the world's wonder.

做女儿的所付出的那种爱,是世上没谁能受得起的——这是世间的奇迹。

October

October 1

Daughters are always astonished to discover that their mother too was once young. A little daft. A little confused. A little awkward. Argumentative, vulnerable, given to falling flat on her face. And so able to understand.

女儿们往往会惊奇地发现,她们的妈妈也曾年轻过。有点傻,有点糊涂,还有点笨拙。也爱与人争辩,也会脆弱不堪,也有一败涂地的时候。于是,她们理解了妈妈。

October

Maybe I haven't done the things I meant to. But I had you. And that is enough. More, far more, than enough.

也许我还没做打算做的事情。但我已经有你了。这就足够了……又岂止是足够啊。

  October

You think you know your daughter – and then she astonishes you. Constantly.

你以为自己了解女儿,她却总能出乎你的意料,向来如此。

October 4

Daughters are a delight. Some of the time. Most of the time. When, that is, they are not putting their white ballet tights into the wash inside black jeans! Daughters!

女儿总是快乐的源泉。大多数时间都是如此。除了她们把芭蕾服跟黑色牛仔裤一股脑儿全扔进洗衣机的时候！小冤家啊！

  October

I share your joys and successes – but never forget I'm here for you when things go wrong.

你收获了喜悦和成功,我们共同分享;但请永远不要忘记,当你遇到坎坷时,我也一直伴你左右。

October 6

Thank you for reawakening wonder.   谢谢你，带来了新的惊喜！

7 October

And I love you still – as when I first held you in my arms. When you first took a step towards me. When you first went to school – and never looked back to wave. All those years that make the lass I love – my dear, my precious girl.

从第一次把你抱在怀里,我便一直无比地爱你。当你蹒跚学步,第一次朝我走来;当你第一次走进学校后,不再回头跟我挥手告别。所有这些时光都见证着你的成长——我爱你,我最亲爱的,我珍贵的女儿。

October 8

A daughter is your part in forever.   女儿便是你生命的延续，永永远远。

A daughter can lead you into a wider world.　　女儿可以带你去瞧瞧更广阔的世界。

October 10

I gave you life, and in consequence, spring days of sun and rain, the slap of water under a dinghy's prow, waterfalls and the high crags.

我给予你生命,然后我们一同走过晴晴雨雨的春日,在小艇的船头戏水玩耍,欣赏过瀑布的壮美风景,也见识了壮观的悬崖绝壁。

11 October

Thank you for all the little astonishments – a tuft of daisies, a small lopsided pot, a painting of us all. A furry toffee. A hug when I've been sad. A song.

感谢你为我制造的小小惊喜——一束雏菊,一个底部有点歪的小锅,一幅全家福,一颗湿漉漉的太妃糖,在我心情沮丧的时候你给我的拥抱,还有你唱给我的歌。

October 12

It is good to share the world with a dear daughter.

与亲爱的女儿一同分享这个世界,感觉好棒啊!

  October

I always knew you were wonderful – but you get better every day.

我一直都知道你非常棒,但是你每天还在一点点进步,变得越来越棒。

October 14

Any mother or father hits new lows but "Luff you" sets all right.

所有的爸爸妈妈都会遭遇人生低谷,但一句"爱你呦"让一切都重回正轨。

No one told you that you would feel in your own heart every pain, every loss, every disappointment, every rebuff, every cruelty that your daughter experiences – life long.

从没有人告诉你，你女儿遭遇的每一次痛苦，每一次失去后的空空如也，每一次失望，每一次受到的冷漠回绝以及残忍对待——你也都会感同身受，并且毕生如此。

October 16

Daughters can be erratic in their correspondence – but when you need them they are there.

女儿嘴上说的可能不那么可靠,但你需要她的时候,她总会陪在你身旁。

17 October

A daughter is a new beginning.   女儿便是新的开始。

October 18

A daughter never ceases to spring surprises. 女儿永远都会给你带来惊喜。

  October

A daughter – a gift to the world.   女儿是赠予整个世界的礼物。

October 20

A daughter always has something new with which to astonish you.

女儿身上总是有些新的亮点,让你大吃一惊,又喜上心头。

  October

A parent holds her like a flower, like thinnest glass. We wonder at this new and lovely life, incredible in its perfection. We grow with her, learning as we go.

我们小心翼翼地把她捧在手心,她如此娇小动人,像美丽的花朵,又像薄薄的易碎的玻璃。这个可爱的新生命完美得令人难以置信,着实让我们感到惊奇。我们同她一起成长,学到新的东西。

October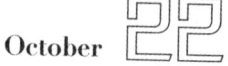

We exasperate one another but that is half the fun. We are part of one another forever and forever.

我们有意无意地惹恼对方,但这也只是生活的一半乐趣。我们已经有了深深的羁绊,生生世世,永永远远。

  October

I am so proud of you. Proud of your courage and your concern for others, your resilience, your love of life. Proud of all that you've achieved. Your creativity. Your willingness to learn – so much in one small person!

我为你感到无比自豪,你有着十足的勇气,会体贴地为别人着想,有着很强的适应能力,热爱生活。我为你感到骄傲,你取得的所有成就,别具一格的创造力,以及对学习的热情与向往。满满的优点集聚于一个小人儿身上,我真是好幸福啊!

October 24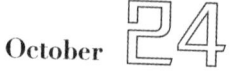

There are only a few things I couldn't do without. And you're one of them.

在我的生命中,只有几件不可或缺的宝贝。你便是其中之一。

  October

May you always find something to delight you.

祝愿你总能找到快乐的源泉。

October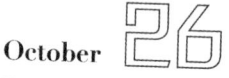

I am so very ordinary. How then did I produce a girl like you? So beautiful, so clever and so kind.

我普通得不能再普通了,却是如此幸运,诞下你这样一个女儿——美丽至极,无比聪慧,又如此友好善良。

  October

We know your strength but – never forget! In case of dire emergency. We're here!

我们知道你很有能力。但是请永远不要忘记,如果不幸陷入岌岌可危的境地,我们永远都在你身边!

October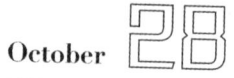

Thanks for all the cards – hand drawn or by Renoir... for all the parcels – knobbly or beribboned.

感谢你送给我的所有卡片——无论是你的手绘还是大师雷诺阿的作品……也感谢你给我的各种礼物——无论是摸上去有点疙疙瘩瘩的,还是有缎带精心装饰的,我通通都喜欢。

  October

Every year you grow more dear to me.　　一年又一年，我越来越爱你。

October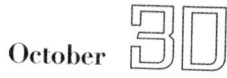

Love encompasses everything – dark and dull and shining gold. She's yours, and you're hers. Forever.

爱包含万物——黑暗的时刻,索然无味的日子以及如金子般璀璨耀眼的生活。她是你的,你也是她的,永永远远。

  October

I loved you as a baby, plump as a piglet, as a school child, awkward and eager, as a teenager, totally confused. And now most of all wise and funny and adventurous – my dearest friend.

我时刻深爱着你——从你还是个婴儿，胖乎乎的像个小猪仔；背上书包踏入校门，有点尴尬，又有点期盼；到了你十几岁的时候，心中充满迷惑与不解；直到现在，你已经无比聪颖、幽默又充满冒险精神——我的女儿，我最亲爱的朋友。

Daughters grow,
change and weave most unexpected lives.
But still the wonder grows –
for in the alteration love persists.

女儿总会成长、改变，编织最意想不到的人生。
纵使她给你的惊喜总在变化，
但对你的爱却始终不变。

FOR MY DAUGHTER

女儿是父母的万花筒

365 Daily Messages of Love

［英］帕姆·布朗 —— 著

新星出版社　NEW STAR PRESS

November

November 1

I could have been rich. I could have been famous but these things are very doubtful. I had you and that was a sure and certain victory.

我有可能会富有,也有可能会出名。但这些事会不会发生终归说不准。现在我有了你,这让我成为了名副其实的人生赢家。

November 2

May you find all the good things you deserve. My dear daughter.

希望你收获所有值得拥有的小美好,我亲爱的女儿。

November 3

Thank you for showing me, when I thought my mothering days were over, that the best days between us are only just beginning.

当我以为你不再需要我的时候,感谢你用行动证明,我们之间最美好的日子才刚刚开始。

November 4

I wish you happy and secure and comfortable and wise. But not yet. Get the adventures in first.

我希望你过得幸福平安,生活舒适并且头脑聪明。但是还没到时候。先迈出你的第一步,踏上人生的冒险之旅吧。

November 5

Daughters are like a very complex recipe. You start off with confidence and hope – then reach a stage of such difficulty that you feel it has all gone horribly and irretrievably wrong. But, at last, you find to your astonishment and delight a totally unexpected transformation.

女儿真是太复杂了!一开始,你胸有成竹,满心期待;然后你会到达某个阶段,面临的艰难险阻让你觉得,一切都大错特错,离谱得无可救药。但是最后,你惊喜地发现,你的女儿经历了蜕变,令你喜出望外。

November 6

The world is yours. Fly free.   全世界都是你的，自由地翱翔吧！

7 November

Our girl. You are grown long since, but still I remember the weight of you across my shoulders, the clasp of your hands about my neck, your laughter in my ears.

我们的女儿啊。虽然你早已长大成人,但我仍记得你跨在我肩膀上的重量,记得你的小手紧紧搂在我脖子上时的温热,记得回荡在我身边的你的笑声。

November 8

So little time ago you ran to me, small arms spread wide and love and laughter in your face. But time is kind. It simply changes joy. I hear your knock and see your smile and am young again.

不久之前,你还像小企鹅一样,支棱着胳膊朝我跑来,脸上洋溢着爱与笑容。但是时间很善良,并没有带走我们的快乐。我听见你敲门,然后看见你面带笑容地站在门口,我仿佛又回到了年轻的时候。

November 9

How strange, how wonderful to find one's daughter understands things beyond one's comprehension. Higher mathematics. Greek. Physics or Cordon Bleu. How to mend a fuse. Or ride a motor bike.

发现女儿懂得比自己还多时,是多么奇特,又多么美妙啊!高数、希腊语、物理还有高级烹饪。她们还知道怎么弄保险丝,还有怎么骑摩托车,真是太厉害啦!

November 10

Your mind is amazed at all the wonders of the world. Grow, my dear daughter, learn and love.

你有一颗好奇的心,想要探索世界上形形色色的东西。快快长大吧,我亲爱的女儿,带着求知的心,努力去爱吧。

11 November

Even in a non-kissy, non-cuddly family invisible cuddles and kisses wrap you round.

即使你的家人都不喜欢亲吻和拥抱,你还是会被无形的亲吻和拥抱包围着。

November 12

Thank you for your vast determination. Your triumphs over gravity. Your mastering of skills. Your trust. Your welcoming. Your love.

谢谢你那坚定的决心,谢谢你努力学会站起来,谢谢你掌握各种技能,谢谢你的信任,谢谢你迎我回家,谢谢你的爱。

13 November

Each day has been a wonder and astonishment.

每一天,你都给我们带来惊喜,让我们生活得有滋有味。

November 14

A father looks forward to the time when he has a daughter – and can make and build with the most amazing care – her very own castle!

父亲总是很期待有个女儿,然后一起搭建属于她的城堡。他此时的精心呵护,没有什么能比得上。

15 November

Now we meet as equals, having forgiven one another, having learned to love, having rediscovered laughter.

现在我们可以平等地沟通,原谅了对方的全部,学会了如何去爱,并且重拾了笑容。

November 16

However sad I am, a note or a text from you brings me happiness.

无论我有多么难过,你的一张纸条或一条短信都会令我幸福。

17 November

A daughter and her mother are so entwined in heart and mind that, gladly or unwillingly, they share each love, each joy, each sorrow and each bitter wrong lifelong.

女儿和妈妈之间已经有了深深的牵绊。无论如何,她们都分享着彼此的爱和快乐,共同承担着悲伤以及做了错事之后的痛苦,一辈子都是如此。

November 18

Daughters never quite forgive you for throwing out the clothes you wore at twenty. Apparently they're in.

如果你把自己二十岁时穿过的衣服都丢掉,那女儿肯定不会打心底里原谅你。显而易见,那些衣服太时髦啦!

19 November

Whether they realize it or not mothers and daughters are still entangled, even into age – and one's pain and joy lives in the other's heart.

母亲和女儿总是惺惺相惜，无论她们是否意识到，但事实就是这样。年复一年，母亲和女儿早已心灵相通，无论是过着称心如意的生活，还是饱受痛苦与煎熬，对方永远都会感同身受。

November 20

As you grew and smiled and began to speak every day brought a new delight.

当你慢慢长大，笑逐颜开，开始咿呀学语，与你共度的每一天，都会给我们带来新的快乐。

21 November

When you were very small you made me plasticine pots and pictures of myself – all hair and smile and skinny legs. Caterpillars and stones. Fluffy toffees. Poems. I have them still. Safe and protected.

当你还很小的时候,你送给我橡皮泥做的小锅,亲手给我画的肖像——我全身都毛茸茸的,脸上有大大的微笑,腿像树枝一样细。还有毛毛虫和小石头,湿漉漉的太妃糖,以及你写给我的诗。我到现在还留着它们,小心翼翼地保存着。

November 22

Love, courage and an enquiring mind. That's what I wish for you. Together with the ability to stand in other people's shoes. And to laugh at yourself.

充满爱与勇气,带着一颗求知的心,这便是我对你的期许。除此之外,你要多多为他人着想,并且笑对人生。

23 November

Here is the ghost of little fingers clasping your hand, here are arms stretched out to greet you; here is a face uplifted for your kiss. The child has grown and gone away – and yet the sweetness stays.

你看那个小魔鬼,小小的手紧紧牵着你;细细的胳膊使劲伸着,就为了和你打招呼;胖乎乎的小脸蛋往你跟前凑,想要你的亲吻。孩子已经长大成人,远走高飞,但是你们之间的甜蜜依旧如初。

November 24

Thank you for the little things – a pat in passing – a snuggle, a hug – a friendly wink, a smile. A cup of tea. Buttered toast. A rose in a milk bottle. The little things that make my life possible.

感谢你为我做的小事——走过我身边时的轻轻一拍，一个暖暖的依偎或拥抱，友好的眨眼，以及甜甜的微笑。一杯茶，一片抹满黄油的吐司，一束插在牛奶瓶里的玫瑰花。你所做的一件件小事，让我的生活充满意义。

November 25

Mothers and fathers never cease to be astonished by their daughters.

爸爸妈妈永远会因为女儿做的事情而收获惊喜。

November 26

I wish for you courage and clear thinking, hope and a happy heart. Always.

我希望你充满勇气,思维清晰,拥抱希望和葆有一颗快乐的心。永远如此。

27 November

What a lot of fuss we make over disappointments and failures and the loss of material things. When all that really matters is that the family have each other – and you.

我们经历的各种失望、失败以及物质上的失去,真是没什么可大惊小怪的。真正重要的,是我们作为家人的互相扶持,尤其是你带来了希望。

November 28

Thank you, dearest, for all the Birthday and Mother's Day Suprizzles. But thank you most of all for the un-birthday remembrances.

谢谢你,我最亲爱的宝贝,为我带来的所有生日和母亲节的惊喜。但最重要的是,感谢你在普普通通的日子里,给我带来的独家记忆。

29 November

However much we disagree. I need your life to interlock with mine, to know you share my secrets and my joys. To know that you are there.

无论我们之间有多大分歧，我需要与你的生活产生深深地连接，让我知道，你分享着我的秘密和喜悦；让我知道，你就在这里。

November 30

A parent and child have a relationship different to any other – whatever loves, whatever hates, lie between them, they are bound together.

父母与孩子之间的关系异于其他——无论他们之间产生了怎样的爱与恨,他们的心永远紧紧相连。

December

December 1

I'm proud of all your achievements. But I'm most proud of your being just you. You are special to me whatever you do.

我为你所有的成就感到自豪。但你最令我欣慰的,是你的独一无二。无论你做什么,对我来说你永远都是世上绝无仅有的瑰宝。

December 2

Your daughter may not become or do the things you dreamed of. She may not become a doctor, a prima ballerina, an archaeologist, a lawyer.

你的女儿可能不会做你之前梦想过的事情——她可能不会成为医生、首席女舞伶、考古学家或者律师。

3 December

Life has been very kind to me. It has given me you.

生活对我真是太善良了，赐予了我你这个小家伙。

December 4

I wish you success that has no sting. I wish you joy and peace and warm contentment. And always, always, love.

我希望你的成功之路上没有荆棘,我希望你过得快乐平安,内心也总是洋溢着满足的喜悦。最重要的,我希望你永远能收获满满的爱。

5 December

My dearest girl – source of silly surprises, unexpected hugs, laughter, comfort.

我最亲爱的女儿——你总是带给我们傻得可爱的惊喜,出其不意的拥抱,欢乐的笑声,还有最贴心的安慰。

December 6

Even the worst of times are balanced out by those of joy, success, sharing and laughter. Days to remember with a happy heart.

即使在那些最黑暗的日子里，看到你过得快乐，取得了傲人的成绩，想起你与我分享的点点滴滴，还有你脸上洋溢的欢笑——我的心里也倍感幸福，那些黑暗也不复存在了。

7 December

You can never be lonely – for our love is always with you.

你永远不会感到孤独,因为我们的爱始终陪伴着你。

December 8

Go where I never dared to go. Live a life worth living.

去看看吧,去那些我从不敢去的地方。活出你的精彩人生吧!

December

You have my love – the love that links us. Take it with you into the world that I will never know.

我永远爱着你——爱将我们紧紧相连。带着我的这份爱,去闯荡我未曾见识过的天地吧!

December 10

You are there for me – however far away you are. We share our highs and lows. You are your own assured and independent self – yet still a part of me. Dear lass. Dear daughter.

无论你在世界的哪个地方,我知道你永远触手可及。我们分享人生的起起落落。你自信独立,但你仍然是我的一部分。亲爱的女儿,你是我最爱的姑娘!

11 December

How could I ever have produced someone so clever, so kind, so loving, so special as you? But how very glad I am that I did.

你冰雪聪明、心地善良又温柔体贴,我是怎么诞下你这样一个独一无二的珍宝呢?但事实就是这样,我心里是多么高兴啊!

December 12

Dear daughter. Live a most happy life – your own. Unique and brave and wonderful.

亲爱的女儿,过最幸福的人生吧。记住——要为自己而活。别具一格、勇敢无畏、精彩绝伦,这便是我对你的期许。

13 December

Thank you for your vast determination. Your mastering of skills. Your trust. Your welcoming. Your love.

谢谢你那坚定的决心,谢谢你掌握各种技能。谢谢你的信任。谢谢你迎我回家。谢谢你的爱。

December 14

…And all of it has combined to make you what you are. Our special daughter. Our loving – and most dearly loved lass.

……所有这一切造就了现在的你。我们独一无二的女儿啊!我们最体贴、最亲爱的姑娘!

☀ ⛅ ☁ 🌧 🌬 🌨 **15** December

Dearest daughter. One tiny tug will have me dropping anything I'm engaged in – you are, above everything, the heartbeat of my life.

我最亲爱的女儿。只要你的小手一拽,我就会放下任何手头上的事情——你比一切都重要,你就是我的心头肉。

December 16

Thank you for all the years you've given us. Years to treasure. Our dearest daughter. Our lovely lass.

谢谢你,这些年给我们带来的美好,我们会将这些日子永远珍藏于心间。我们最亲爱的女儿,我们最可爱的姑娘!

17 December

Thank you for all the prezzies – serious and silly. Scent and stockings, rose bushes, kumquats, tea and chocolate mice. Fine paintings. Ginger and liquorice. Garlic and poppadoms. Yo-yos and teddy bears.

感谢你送来的所有礼物——无论是正式隆重的,还是傻得可爱的。香水、长筒袜、大捧玫瑰花、小金橘、茶叶和巧克力小老鼠;精心制作的画;生姜和甘草;大蒜和印度薄饼;溜溜球和泰迪熊。

December 18

I am continually amazed by you – my lovely, unpredictable daughter.

你总是能不断地带给我惊喜,我最可爱、最捉摸不透的女儿。

December 19

You are a kaleidoscope. Constantly changing. Always new. The patterns shift but always fascinate. Beautiful. Strange. Bewildering. But always you.

你就是个万花筒,不断地变化,却又总让人耳目一新。图案虽不尽相同,却总是令人着迷。时而美丽动人,时而令人不解,时而又让人手足无措。但你始终是你,这一点可没有变化啊。

December 20

How clever you are. How beautiful. How kind. But, best of all how loving.

我的女儿啊,你是如此冰雪聪明,美丽动人又心地善良,但最重要的是,你的关怀无微不至。

21 December

When all the world is dreary, I think about my daughter, her brightness and her laughter, and life comes right again.

当整个世界变得枯燥乏味时,我会想我的女儿,她是那样的朝气蓬勃,笑得那样灿烂动人,我的生活又充满了前进的动力。

December 22

It's good when a mother and her daughter store things in their minds to tell each other. People they've met, things they've done, delights... Small threads that bind them together in love and understanding.

妈妈和女儿会收集生活中的点点滴滴——见到的人、做过的事、收获的快乐……然后与对方一同分享。这些故事就像细细的线将她们紧紧联系在一起，传递着爱与理解。

23 December

You have to fight your own battles, love. But I'm here in your corner with the bucket and sponge.

你必须亲自迎接前方的战斗,我最亲爱的女儿。但我永远都是你坚强的后盾,随时为你补充能量,为你加油助威。

December 24

If I could give you anything it would be a quietness at the very heart of your life that would remain tranquil and certain whatever befell.

如果我还能给你们什么的话,那就是在你们生活的中心投下一片静谧。无论发生什么,这份静谧会让你们保持平静。

25 December

Most of all I wish you courage… 最重要的是，我希望你能不畏艰险，勇往直前……

December 26

Whenever you meet beauty, we are beside you. You can never be lonely – for our love is always with you.

无论何时,当你遇见了美好的人事物,我们都在你身旁。你永远不是一个人,因为我们的爱总与你相随。

27 December

Whatever happens... our lives are stitched together by a thread of gold that cannot change, whatever changes come.

无论发生什么……我们的生命已经紧紧用一根金线捆绑在一起,坚不可摧。就算世事多变,我们的爱也亘古不变。

December 28

May you know friendship. May you know love.

希望你能拥有情深似海的友谊。希望你能感受到深入人心的爱。

29 December

My wishes for you. The true joy of love is only shaped by time. I wish you that discovery, that happiness.

我希望你知道,爱所产生的快乐是靠时间一点点累积的。我希望你勇于探索,并且拥有幸福人生。

December 30

Gather up your courage, your talents and your dreams. Be determined. Face your fears. Cling on to hope. And if you fail, get up and go on running. I wish you joy – in love. In life.

亲爱的女儿,鼓起勇气,大步向前吧!你才华横溢,奋力去追逐自己的梦想吧!坚定信念,直面恐惧,怀揣希望,永不放弃。如果你跌倒了,那么重新站起来,继续向前冲吧!我希望你生活幸福——感受到满满的爱,并且永远快乐。

31 December

We remember all the days that are gone, and the joy you have given us – and we look forward to the joy to come. Bless you always.

我们记得过去的每个日夜,也记得你给我们带来的所有欢笑。时光易逝,而我们也期待着未来与你共同经历的幸福与快乐。愿上天永远保佑你。

For My Daughter 365 Daily Messages of Love
Published in 2016 by Helen Exley Giftbooks in Great Britain.
Edited by Helen Exley
Words by Pam Brown © Helen Exley Creative Ltd 2016
Illustrated by Juliette Clarke © Helen Exley Creative Ltd 2016.
Design, selection and arrangement © Helen Exley Creative Ltd 2016

The moral right of the author has been asserted. A copy of the CIP data is available from the British Library on request. All rights reserved. No part of this publication may be reproduced or transmitted in any form or by any means, electronic or mechanical, including photocopy, recording or any information storage and retrieval system without permission in writing from the Publisher. Printed in China.
www.helenexleygiftbooks.com

The Simplified Chinese translation rights are arranged through RR Donnelley Asia
Simplified Chinese edition copyright: 2020 New Star Press Co., Ltd.
All rights reserved.

著作版权合同登记号：01-2019-5503

图书在版编目（CIP）数据

女儿是父母的万花筒：汉英对照／（英）帕姆·布朗著．－－北京：新星出版社，2020.12

ISBN 978-7-5133-4175-2

Ⅰ．①女… Ⅱ．①帕… Ⅲ．①英语－汉语－对照读物 ②格言－汇编－世界 Ⅳ．① H319.4：H

中国版本图书馆 CIP 数据核字（2020）第 200538 号

女儿是父母的万花筒

[英] 帕姆·布朗　著

策划编辑：李金学	**责任编辑**：姜　淮
特约编辑：赵　丹	**责任校对**：刘　义
责任印制：李珊珊	**装帧设计**：赵宇飞

出版发行：新星出版社
出 版 人：马汝军
社　　址：北京市西城区车公庄大街丙3号楼　　100044
网　　址：www.newstarpress.com
电　　话：010-88310888
传　　真：010-65270449
法律顾问：北京市岳成律师事务所

读者服务：010-88310811　　service@newstarpress.com
邮购地址：北京市西城区车公庄大街丙 3 号楼　　100044

印　　刷：北京尚唐印刷包装有限公司
开　　本：889mm×1194mm　　1/32
印　　张：13.25
字　　数：50千字
版　　次：2020年12月第一版　　2020年12月第一次印刷
书　　号：ISBN 978-7-5133-4175-2
定　　价：48.00元（全六册）

版权专有，侵权必究；如有质量问题，请与印刷厂联系调换。

To have a daughter to us it is a miracle.
Greatest of gifts.
Dearest of daughters.

女儿,

是生命的奇迹,

是最好的礼物,

是父母爱的归宿。